THIS BOOK
BELONGS TO

....

....

Thank you for Purchasing my book and taking the time to read it from front to back. I am always grateful when a reader chooses my work and I hope you enjoyed it!

With the vast selection available online, I am touched that you chose to be purchasing my work and take valuable time out of your life to read it. My hope is that you feel you made the right decision.

I very much would like to know what you thought of the book. Please take the time to write an honest and informative review on Amazon.com. Your experience and opinions will be of great benefit to me and those readers looking to make an informed choice.

With much thanks.

@COPYRIGHT 2024

The content contained within this book may not be reproduced, duplicated, or transmitted without direct written permission from the author or the publisher. Under no circumstances will any blame or legal responsibility be held against the publisher, or author, for any damages, reparation, or monetary loss due to the information contained within this book. Either directly or indirectly.

Legal Notice:
This book is copyright protected. This book is only for personal use. You cannot amend, distribute, sell, use, quote, or paraphrase any part, or the content within this book, without the consent of the author or publisher.

Disclaimer Notice:
Please note the information contained within this document is for educational and entertainment purposes only. All effort has been executed to present accurate, up-to-date, and reliable, complete information. No warranties of any kind are declared or implied. Readers acknowledge that the author is not engaging in the rendering of legal, financial, medical, or professional advice. The content within this book has been derived from various sources. Please consult a licensed professional before attempting any techniques outlined in this book. By reading this document, the reader agrees that under no circumstances is the author responsible for any losses, direct or indirect, which are incurred as a result of the use of the information contained within this document, including, but not limited to — errors, omissions, or inaccuracies.

Table of Contents

Introduction	5
Rationale for Establishing a Peer Mediation Program	8
Part 1: History of Conflict Resolution	9
Part 2: Steps for Implementing a Peer Mediation Program	26
Part 3: Ready to Use Templates with Links to FREE PDF/Word Docs Templates A - CC	37

Introduction

A school's primary mission is to ensure that students achieve their fullest academic potential in a safe and nurturing environment. We need to create a safe-school climate where students feel connected and protected. Teaching students to get along with their peers is part of creating a safe- school climate. When students learn how to resolve their conflicts in a peaceful manner, the atmosphere at school can be more pleasant for everyone. In a safe-school environment teachers can teach and students can learn.

According to Susan Colville-Hall, Ph.D., the characteristics of the school culture and climate that protect students include the following:
- Positive school climate and atmosphere;
- High performance expectations for all students;
- Inclusionary values and practices throughout the school;
- Strong student association with the school community and the learning process;
- High levels of student participation in the schooling process;
- High level of parent involvement in the schooling process; and
- Equity in opportunities for academic skill acquisition and social development.
- Teaching students to get along with their peers is a part of creating a safe-school climate. Conflict is a normal part of everyday life, therefore, a natural part of school life. Conflict resolution is a problem-solving approach that teaches one to look at the problem through a series of steps and to mutually decide upon a resolution.

Why do schools need a Peer Mediation Program?

According to the National Association for Mediation in Education (NAME), five of the most common purposes of a school mediation program are:
1. to increase communication among students, teachers, administrators, and parents.
2. to reduce school violence, vandalism, and suspensions.
3. to encourage children, adolescents, and teens to resolve their own disputes by developing listening, critical thinking, and problem-solving skills.
4. to teach peaceful resolution of differences, a skill needed to live in a multicultural world.
5. to motivate students' interest in conflict resolution, justice, and the American legal system, and encourage active citizenship.

Development and implementation of a Peer Mediation Program is one way to teach students to resolve conflict in a peaceful manner. When students learn how to resolve their own conflict, the atmosphere at school can be more pleasant for everyone. The school would be better able to focus on its original mission – Academic Achievement.

All skills require practice to master, and peer mediation enables students to develop their conflict resolution skills where it matters most – on real-life conflicts. Mediating real conflicts at school also encourages the transfer to life outside of school.

This book is divided into three main parts:
Part 1: History of Conflict Resolution
Part 2. Steps for Implementing a Peer Mediation Program
Part 3: Ready to Use Templates A – CC

Why did I create this book? Because… I know Peer Mediation works! I would love to see a Peer Mediation program in your school.

It is my hope that this book will assist you in implementing a Peer Mediation program in your school community.

Best wishes,

Rationale for Establishing a Peer Mediation Program

1. Conflict is a natural state often accompanying changes in our schools' growth. It is better approached with skills than avoidance.
2. More appropriate and effective systems are needed to deal with conflict in a school setting than expulsions, suspensions, or court interventions.
3. The use of mediation to resolve school-based disputes can result in improved communication between and among students, teachers, and administrators. In general, school climate can improve.
4. The use of mediation as a conflict resolution method can result in a reduction of violence, vandalism, chronic school absence, and suspension.
5. Mediation training helps both young people and teachers to better understand themselves and others.
6. Mediation training increases students' interest in conflict resolution, justice, and the American legal system.
7. Shifting the responsibility for solving nonviolent conflicts to students frees the adults to concentrate more on teaching and less time on discipline.
8. Conflict resolution training increases skills in listening, critical thinking, and problem solving – skills basic to all learning.
9. Conflict resolution education emphasizes seeing other points of view and resolving differences peacefully – skills that assist one to live in a multicultural world.
10. Mediation provides problem solving tools that are well suited to the problems that young people face. Students can solve their problems for which they would not seek adult help (Colorado School Mediation Project and Conflict Resolution Education: A Guide to Implementing Programs in Schools, Youth-Serving Organizations, and Community Juvenile Justice Settings).

Part 1: History of Conflict Resolution

History of Conflict Resolution Education

In order to fully understand the concepts of conflict resolution and its role in education and society, there is a need to review what is being said and implemented by educators and experts in the field of conflict resolution research. Conflict resolution education literature is reviewed in this section to give direction to this work and to aid in the interpretation of the findings. First, the topic of conflict resolution education is discussed, focusing on its history, programs, philosophy, and curriculum. Second, the research on conflict resolution program implementation is reviewed to determine what steps are critical to the effective implementation of a Conflict Resolution/Peer Mediation Program at the middle school level.

Since the beginning of time, human beings have created a variety of options for resolving their conflicts. History reveals violence as a consistent way of resolving conflict. Conflict resolution is a problem solving approach that teaches students and staff to look at the problem through a series of steps that clarify the problem and, hopefully, result in a resolution. Mediation is a process for resolving disputes and conflicts in which a neutral third party acts as a mediator. In mediation, trained student mediators help their classmates find solutions to their conflicts. Peer mediation is not about finding out who is right or wrong. Not every problem is suitable for peer mediation. Common problems involving name calling, rumors, and students bumping into other students in the hallways have been successfully resolved through peer mediation most of the time.

In the following list are the ground rules for the mediation process. When both students agree to the ground rules, the mediation can proceed.

Ground Rules

Participants should be willing to:
- Solve the problem
- Tell the truth
- Listen without interrupting
- Be respectful
- Take responsibility for carrying out the agreement
- Keep the situation confidential

Mediation Steps:
- Agree upon the ground rules
- Each student tells his/her story
- Discuss the stories
- Have each student put himself/herself into the other student's shoes
- Generate solutions
- Discuss solutions
- Select a solution
- Sign a contract or an agreement

In general, the field of Conflict Resolution Education has emerged from a variety of theoretical backgrounds, including social justice concerns, advocates of nonviolence and peace education, and law-related education projects. Recently, conflict resolution education has been influenced by the school reform movement which seeks to empower students by including them in decision-making and the problem solving process. There appears to be an interrelationship between creating a safe cooperative school climate and improved academic performance (Arends, 1998: Joyce, Hersh, Hartoonian, 1993). According to Jensen (1998), excess stress and threats in the school environment may be the single greatest contributor to impaired academic learning. This information indicates that student safety and learning are closely related, and unless staff and students feel safe, neither teaching nor learning will occur. Kaplan claims principals must structure their schools' learning environments with high expectations for achievement and behavior and for positive relationships among students and teachers to ensure safer, more inclusive, and higher achieving schools. Students have many developmental needs that a safe and strong instructional climate can address (Kaplan and Owings, 2000). To perform at their best, students must:

- Feel physically and emotionally safe
- Believe they are part of a valued group
- Experience the status and respect that comes with showing social, academic, or co-curricular competence
- Have opportunities to learn and do meaningful things that make a difference in their world
- Be encouraged to better know themselves by challenging, questioning, and reflecting on events
- Connect with caring adult role models to help them answer major life questions
- Feel invested and engaged in learning they believe is interesting, valuable, and worthwhile.

Social Justice Concerns

Conflict resolution programs in schools grew out of the social justice concerns of the 1960s and 1970s. Several community-based dispute resolution centers emerged across the United States and Canada. Some groups, such as the Quakers, had long supported the teaching of problem solving and peacemaking to young children. A broad spectrum of religious and peace activists adopted this cause in the mid-1970s. The process of mediation is based on the concept of win/win solutions. Teachers began incorporating dispute resolution instruction into their curriculum.

Community Mediation Centers

Peer mediation programs as we know it are modeled after the community mediation centers of the 1980s (Roderick, 1988). Citizens generated their solutions to interpersonal and neighborhood conflicts in the community mediation centers. They tried to assist disputants to reach agreements through mediation rather than litigation. These centers, which are typically nonprofit community-based agencies, use trained community volunteers to provide a wide range of mediation services to youth and adults

Law Students Use Alternative Dispute Resolution

As citizens were going to community mediation centers, students on college campuses began to govern their own schools through law-related education projects. There was a growing use of mediation and alternative dispute resolution (ADR) on college campuses. Today many small claims courts offer mediation before cases are brought before judges. Law schools have begun to teach future attorneys the principles of ADR. In turn, law students are teaching ADR skills to students in the public school setting, such as the project that was implemented at Dominion Middle School in 1999.

A collaboration between The Ohio State University College of Law's Dispute Resolution Program, Squire, Sanders & Dempsey LLP, and Dominion Middle School occurred to bring the "Dispute Resolution and Youth Taking Negotiation to the Youth of Columbus" project to the students of Dominion Middle School. Forty-five law students presented the program in a series of six forty-minute sessions. The lessons were taught to all students during their reading/language arts block. The following is a curriculum overview as described by Kassar and Ray. The first three lessons of the program deal with conflict resolution skills, as these are essential building blocks for learning how to negotiate. The key conflict resolution topics include:

recognizing and managing emotions, learning about perceptions, exploring empathy, learning about listening skills, and the basic value of respecting others. The next two lessons are designed to begin to apply skills to the art of negotiation. The students will learn how to set goals to solve their problems, brainstorm options for potential solutions, and evaluate those options and choose the best solution. During the final lesson, students will conduct an actual negotiation or mediation. They also learn how to develop a back-up plan in case no agreement/solution could be reached. The attorneys from Squire, Sanders, & Dempsey LLP, helped the students to prepare for their negotiation. According to the questionnaire the teachers and students completed, the "Dispute Resolution" project which was very successful at Dominion Middle School. One limitation existed because only 90% of the student body received the project due to the conflicting class schedules of the law students. The law students returned to Dominion Middle School the next school year to present the project to the new sixth grade students.

National Association for Mediation in Education (NAME)

In 1984, a group of educators, activists, and community mediators came together and created a group of the diverse movements within the field on conflict resolution. They formed the National Association for Mediation in Education (NAME) at the University of Massachusetts at Amherst. NAME became a support network and materials clearinghouse for schools attempting to promote constructive conflict resolution programs. When NAME was first established in 1984, there were only a half dozen well-developed peer mediation programs. By 1988, the number grew to 200. Now the number of well-developed programs goes into the thousands. NAME knows there are many important factors to consider when

developing and implementing a peer mediation program. NAME considers the following key elements to be vital to a good program:
- Good mediation training,
- A mediation team that represents the student body, and
- Strong staff support.

NAME (1993) suggests that middle school peer mediators receive 12–15 hours of training. NAME suggests the following training session content:

Conflict – Discussion of what it is, different styles of dealing with it, and the types of conflict that exist.

Communication styles – Non-verbal communication, assertion messages, and "I" statements.

Active listening skills – Good/bad listening techniques, open-ended questions, neutral language, etc.

Mediation process – Learning what it is, the steps involved, confidentiality, etc.

Ongoing/follow-up training such as bias awareness, cultural diversity, and issues of power.

NAME Merges

In December 1995, NAME merged with the National Institute for Dispute Resolution (NIDR) and became the Conflict Resolution Education Network (CREnet) at NIDR. CREnet, formerly NAME, is the primary national and international clearinghouse for information, resources, and technical assistance in the field of conflict resolution and education. It continues to promote the development and implementation of school and university- based conflict resolution programs and curricula.

Developmental and Social Psychology

According to Johnson and Johnson (1996), the concept of the conflict resolution and peer mediation programs is rooted in development and social psychological theory. Students at the middle school level value peer relationships highly and are heavily influenced by them. Therefore, it is important to know student perceptions about the peer mediation process. How students perceive peer mediation influences the choices they make. For peer mediation to be an option for conflict resolution, student perceptions must be positive. If students feel that using the peer mediation process will cause them to lose face with their peers, they will probably not use it (Robinson, Smith & Daunic).

Students who learn positive coping skills have a greater chance of growing into emotionally healthy adults. Successful coping requires that they learn new approaches to challenging situations when what they have been doing stops working. Development psychologists call this process creating new cognitive structures accommodation (Berger, 1994).

Problem Solving Skills

Conflict with peers is a significant source of challenge for middle school students (Kauffman, 1993). Teaching students problem solving skills through a school-wide conflict resolution program that includes peer mediation will help them resolve the inevitable conflicts they will encounter in school. Peer mediation allows students to have a "say" in how their disputes will be resolved.

An effective peer mediation program can improve school climate. One study reported that a Conflict Resolution/Peer Mediation program at the middle school level appeared to produce a positive increase in teachers' ratings of student attitudes about school discipline (Van Slyck & Stern, 1991). The more comprehensive approaches seek to change not only the individual conflict behavior, but to also create a safer, more caring and just school culture (LeBlanc, Lacey & Mulder, 1998).

The six steps in the problem solving process are:
1. Set the stage.
2. Gather perspectives.
3. Identify interests.
4. Create options.
5. Evaluate options.
6. Generate agreement.

Conflict Resolution Education Overview

Although conflict resolution programs may not all look alike, or use identical problem solving models, they do share several basic philosophical ideas.

Conflict is natural. Conflict, to differing degrees, occurs daily in everyone's life. Conflict is not necessarily good or bad. The way conflict is handled makes the outcome a positive or negative experience. If conflict is not handled effectively, it can quickly escalate to physical or emotional violence. If conflict is handled effectively, it can serve as a valuable learning experience.

Individuals can learn new skills. Conflict resolution programs have proven that young people and adults can quickly learn to use effective problem solving concepts and skills. If they are given the opportunity to use their skills in real life situations, they become empowered.

Ideally, all students, school personnel, parents, and community members who work with youth would receive conflict management training. This goal cannot be accomplished immediately, but it should be a long-term goal. The more individuals who are trained in conflict management skills, the more likely it is that the skills will be valued, modeled, and encouraged in conflict situations. The support of the school administration is essential to the success of the conflict management program (Ohio Commission on Dispute Resolution & Conflict Management).

Conflict Resolution Education: Four Approaches

The purpose of conflict resolution education is to provide an environment in which each learner can feel physically and psychologically free from threats and danger. Students can find opportunities to work and learn with others for the mutual achievement of all. The diversity of the school's population is respected and celebrated. Three essential processes of conflict resolution include negotiation, mediation, and consensus of decision making. The four basic approaches to conflict resolution education include:

1. Process Curriculum
2. Peer Mediation
3. Peaceable Classrooms
4. Peaceable Schools

Process Curriculum Approach

Teachers who devote a specific time, a separate course, a distinct curriculum, or a daily lesson to the principles and problem solving processes of conflict resolution are implementing the Process

Curriculum Approach (Creating Safe and Drug-Free Schools: An Action Guide). The Program for Young Negotiators, based on the Harvard Negotiation Project, is representative of this approach. Students, staff, and administrators are taught to practice negotiation skills as a means of goal achievement and dispute resolution. When teachers complete their basic curriculum in the classroom, they are presented with a number of follow-up opportunities. Parents and teachers reported less need to intervene in conflicts.

The Peace Education Foundation (PEF) based in Florida offers a grade level specific curriculum for prekindergarten through grade 12. The PEF goals are to make schools safe, improve school climate, and make instructional strategies more effective. The content of the PEF curriculum is grouped into six components:
1. Community building: Establishing trust, exploring common interests, and respecting differences.
2. Understanding conflict: Identifying conflict, the elements of conflict, escalation and de-escalation of conflict, and different conflict management styles.
3. Perception: Understanding different points of view, enhancing empathy, and increase tolerance.
4. Anger management: Understanding the pros and cons of anger, anger triggers, and anger styles.
5. Rules for Fighting Fair: Learning the rules that provide a framework for appropriate behavior. It is important to learn to focus on the problem, attacking the problem, not the person.
6. These rules are central to the PEF conflict resolution program because they are the principles of nonviolent conflict resolution that promote a peaceful environment.

Teachers facilitate the process of the PEF conflict resolution curriculum by using five strategies:
1. Model: The goal is to let students know how, in "real life," to use the Rules for Fighting Fair.

2. Teach: Teach the students what to do and why. Give them a chance to practice the skills through role-play.
3. Coach: Assist the students in using the techniques appropriately in real-life situations.
4. Encourage: Remind students to use their skills. The goal is for students to behave appropriately without depending on adults.
5. Delegate: After students learn the skills, let them teach or coach less experienced students

Mediation Approach

Under this approach, specially trained student mediators work with their peers to resolve conflicts. Mediation programs reduce the use of traditional disciplinary actions such as detentions and both in-school and out-of-school suspensions. The following guidelines were developed by The Interfaith Center for Peace in Columbus, Ohio.

Mediation is a process used to get disputants to talk about their problem. A neutral third party assists them. The two disputants begin to communicate and are encouraged to find their own solutions. Mediators generally work in teams of two. In mediation a problem is solved non-violently in a win-win situation with each side getting its needs met.

Mediation is appropriate when:
- The disputants want to solve the problem.
- The solution is negotiable.
- The disputants can mediate as equals.

Mediators are the facilitators of the process. Mediators are not judges, detectives, nor counselors. Effective mediators:
- Can remain calm in stressful situations.

- Can remain impartial.
- Help without judging.
- Work as part of a team.
- Must be good listeners.
- Must be able to read body language.
- Must remain in control.
- Must keep things confidential.
- Must be able to direct the mediation without rushing or delaying it.

Mediators have these skills and knowledge:
- Excellent knowledge of the mediation phases
- Good communication
    - Ability to ask questions to clarify
    - Ability to re-word comments without adding or slanting
    - Ability to give instructions
    - Ability to identify the problem
    - Ability to recognize feelings
- Ease in establishing the professional, yet comfortable atmosphere
- Teamwork and team building
- Problem solving
- An awareness of what makes a good solution.

Peaceable Classroom Approach

The Peaceable Classroom is a whole-classroom approach that integrates conflict resolution into the curriculum and daily management of the classroom. The Educators for Social Responsibility (ESR) curriculum, "Making Choices about Conflict, Security, and Peacemaking," is a peaceable classroom approach to conflict resolution. The program teaches teachers how to integrate conflict resolution into curriculum, classroom management, and discipline practices.

ESR defines the term peaceable as meaning a safe, caring, respectful, and productive learning environment. It emphasizes opportunities to practice cooperation, appreciation of diversity, and caring effective communication.

A major premise of ESR is that teachers learn to model the behavior they teach through direct instruction. ESR recommends that students and teachers make decisions together about classroom norms at the beginning of the school year (Education World: 2001. Curriculum: Conflict Resolution Education: Four Approaches).

In peaceful classrooms students learn to manage and resolve conflict on their own by learning to:
- Understand and analyze conflict.
- Understand peace and peacemaking.
- Recognize the role of perceptions and biases.
- Identify feelings.
- Identify factors that cause escalation.
- Handle anger and other feelings appropriately.
- Improve listening skills.
- Improve verbal communication skills.
- Identify common interests.
- Brainstorm multiple options that address interests.
- Evaluate the consequences of different options.
- Create a win-win agreement.

Peaceable School Approach

A peaceable school promotes a climate where everyone uses conflict resolution skills. The Resolving Conflict Creatively Program (RCCP) involves five components:
- Professional development for teachers and other staff
- Regular classroom instruction based on a K-12 curriculum

- Peer mediation
- Administrator training
- Parent training

Schools agree to implement the RCCP curriculum for at least a year before beginning a peer mediation program (Education World: (2001). Curriculum: Conflict Resolution Education: Four Approaches.

There are six fundamental skill areas to Creating a Peaceable School (Patten).
1. **Building a peaceable climate** – Teachers need to develop a classroom environment conducive to conflict resolution management.
2. **Understanding conflict** – Conflict arises when one or more of the following basic needs identified by William Glasser (1984) go unmet:
   - The need for belonging – fulfilled by loving, sharing, and cooperating with others
   - The need for power – fulfilled by achieving, accomplishing, and being recognized and respected
   - The need for freedom – fulfilled by making choices in our lives
   - The need for fun – fulfilled by laughing and playing.
3. **Understanding peace and peacemaking** – In the peaceful school, peace is viewed as a behavior rather than an outcome or goal. The basic principles are intended to separate the people from the problem.
4. **Mediation** – Mediation is a process in which a neutral third party or mediator helps disputants resolve their conflicts peaceably. In the peaceful school, mediation is used within the classroom and school-wide for resolving conflicts.
5. **Negotiation** – Negotiation is a process in which the disputants communicate directly with each other, rather than using a mediator. In a peaceful school, students learn the skills to communicate their thoughts and feelings about a conflict situation.
6. **Group problem solving** – This strategy is used when a conflict affects several members of a group. The two basic principles are:

- The discussion is always directed toward solving the problem.
- The solution never includes punishment or fault finding.

The Creating a Peaceful School program will not work if the staff members view it as another duty they have to do. Staff must be willing to make a commitment to the long-term goals of the program.

Definition of Terms

Key words used in this book include:

Body Language: Nonverbal messages communicated by our bodies

Common Ground: Shared interests; points or things that disputants agree upon

Confidential: Private; not discussed outside the mediation session

Conflict: A disagreement; an argument

Data: Facts; information about an event

De-escalate: To lower the intensity of a conflict

Disputant: A person who is involved in a dispute or conflict

Dispute: An argument, a quarrel

Empathy: Experiencing the feelings, thoughts, or attitudes of another person

Escalate: To make a conflict worse

Fighting Fair: Using peaceful methods to solve a conflict

Fouls: Unfairness in words or actions

Negotiate: To deal or bargain with another, to make an agreement

Neutral Party: A person who doesn't take sides

Paraphrase: To listen to what a person says and then repeat the main idea

Peer Mediation: A method of solving conflicts using a neutral third person

Peer Mediator: A neutral third person who conducts the mediation

Perception: The way a person sees a situation
Resolve: To find a solution to a conflict
Rumor: A statement passed from one person to another without proof
Trigger: An act or event that causes a reaction
Voluntary: A person can choose to participate or not to participate in mediation
Win-Win Solution: A solution that satisfies both parties

Part 2: Steps for Implementing a Peer Mediation Program

Step 1. Confirm the Support of the Administration.
Strong support provided by the administrative personnel is critical to an effective Peer Mediation program. The administration must be willing to provide the support and resources to make the program successful.

Step 2. Select Program Coordinators. Coordinators
Responsibilities (Source: Colorado School Mediation Project):
- Oversee program and decide on how to share responsibilities
- Select a trainer for the CR/PM program
- Introduce staff to the mediation program. **(Template A)**
- Design a process for staff to follow in referring mediation cases
- **(Template B)**
- Select a date for the training; secure a location for the training
- Recruit students to apply to become mediators **(Templates C & D)** All students must have parental consent to participate in the program.
- Select students who will be trained as mediators. **(Templates E & F)** (The trainees should be a diverse group that represents a cross section of the school community.)
- Provide resources to staff about the mediation program **(Template G)**
- Advertise and promote the mediation program (Newsletters, Staff Handbooks, Student Handbooks, Flyers, Posters, Website, etc.)
- **(Templates H & I)**
- Decide when and where mediators will work
- Decide how often mediators will work
- Copy all forms for use (Peer Mediation Script, Agreement Form, Brainstorming Form, Disputant Evaluation Form, Peer Mediator Evaluation Form **(Templates R, S, T, U, V, W, Y, Z, AA, BB)**
- Receive referrals and schedule mediations **(Template S)**
- Receive agreements and monitor follow-up
- Debrief mediations with mediators
- Schedule meetings for ongoing training and support
- Provide link between staff and administration and mediator

- Recruit and train new mediators
- Keep statistical and evaluative information on the program **(Templates AA, BB)**
- Plan orientation sessions for staff, students, and parents
- Conduct program assessment/evaluation
- Organize celebration and recognition program **(Template O)**

Step 3. Develop Building Wide/Community Support for the Program

A Peer Mediation program must be perceived as fulfilling the needs of staff, students, and parents. At least 80% of the staff, both certified and classified, should support the implementation of the program.

Peer Mediation Program Benefits
(Source: Colorado School Mediation Project)

Benefits for School Staff:
- They spend less time settling disputes among students.
- The program allows teachers to spend more time on instruction.
- The program reduces tension among staff and students.
- The program improves the overall school climate.

Benefits for Student Mediators:
- They develop leadership.
- They enhance their language skills.
- They improve their academic achievement.
- They increase their self-esteem.
- They learn valuable communication skills.
- They learn problem solving techniques.
- They have a positive influence on other students.

Benefits for the Student Body:
- They become active in the problem solving process.
- The program provides positive models for solving conflicts.

- Students recognize that adult intervention is not always necessary.
- The process encourages students to share their feelings.
- The program helps to create a greater commitment to making solutions work.

Benefits for Families:
- The problem solving process carries over to families. Parents and students report that conflicts at home are being resolved more effectively.

Benefits for Society:
- Schools that teach students positive ways to resolve conflicts are helping to reduce violence in society.
- Students who learn the skills to resolve conflict positively are likely to do the same when they are adults.

Step 4. Confirm Your Training and Implementation Team.
This team will oversee and directly supervise the mediation program. Team members will determine peer mediator selection, program logistics, and debrief mediators after the mediation is concluded.

Step 5. Develop a Three-Year Action Plan.
It is important to make an initial three-year commitment to the Peer Mediation program. An action plan needs to be developed to explain how the program will operate to meet its goals and objectives. A plan typically spells out:
1. The tasks or steps that need to be accomplished to implement a program.
2. Who will have the responsibility for carrying out the tasks, and
3. A time line for accomplishing the tasks.

Other areas that can be addressed:

What kinds of conflict are appropriate to be referred to mediation?
How common are the conflicts?
How are conflicts usually dealt with?
Is there enough staff support to implement a peer mediation program?
What are the concerns about starting a peer mediation program?
Are there experts available to help with training and program implementation?
What resources are available to support the program?
How will the peer mediation program be evaluated?
How will you know if the program is successful?

Step 6. Select Students to Be Peer Mediators.

- All students should be given the opportunity to apply to become a peer mediator. Each applicant needs to submit a short application telling why he or she would like to become a peer mediator. Each student application needs to have the parent's signature when it is turned in. The student must be willing to make up any missed work and maintain a 2.5 GPA. **(Templates C & D)**
- All staff members should have the opportunity to participate in the peer mediator selection process. A form listing all students who had applied to become mediators will be given to all staff members. Staff members will be asked to give feedback about each student they know. **(Templates E & F)**
- Students who were selected to become peer mediators are given a congratulations letter which should also include the training schedule. **(Template J)**
- Students who were not selected to become peer mediators are given a letter thanking them for their interest. **(Template K)**

Step 7. Prepare for Student Mediation Training.

- Set dates, time, and place.
- Design the training agenda, prepare packets, handouts, & certificates.

- Confirm release time for student mediators.
- Provide snacks.

Step 8. Train Student Mediators.
The training of mediators involves 12- 15 hours. The training should consist of the following components:
- Overview of the mediation process
- Program history
- Understanding the nature of conflict
- Types of conflict mediators are being trained to mediate
- Role plays and learning the script **(Template T)**
- Record keeping and evaluation **(Templates X, Y, Z, AA, BB)**
- Peer Mediator Contract **(Template L)**

Step 9. Design Student Mediation Schedule and Confirm Teacher's Permission.
- Mediators are selected to conduct mediations on "an as needed basis." Student mediators take turns performing mediations and a form is completed as each mediator begins the mediations. **(Template Q)**
- Each student mediator signs a contract to maintain satisfactory school conduct and to maintain satisfactory grades in all classes. **(Template L)**
- Year 2 and beyond: Eighth grade student trainers and mentors must have teacher approval to help with the mediation training. **(Template M)**
- Each student mediator must have teacher approval to participate in a mediation. A teacher has the right to not let a peer mediator participate. A peer mediator also has the right to decline participation in mediation if he or she needs to take a test or complete a class assignment. **(Template N)**

Step 10. Pay Attention to Logistics.
The protocol for making referrals and scheduling mediations is also an important factor in successful program implementation.
- All staff should follow the peer mediation referral process **(Template B)**

- Mediation referrals may be made by teachers, counselors, students, administrators, parents, bus drivers, etc.
- Any non-physical conflict may be referred to mediation. If it is determined the referral is not appropriate for peer mediation, the mediation will be stopped.
- The mediations will occur in a mediation room near the counselor's office or near another support person.
- The school counselor and/or school administrators will intervene in the mediation if help is requested.
- A large group of trained mediators should reduce the amount of class time any one mediator would miss.
- A teacher has the right to refuse to release a mediator or disputant.
- When a mediation is referred, check with both disputants to make sure they both want to go to mediation.
- Once the disputants have confirmed they want to go to mediation, a peer mediator is called to start the process. The mediator who is selected may select another mediator to work with.

Step 11. Orient the Student Body to the Program.

Students need to be aware that the program exists. Involve the student mediators in designing and planning the orientation.

- "Student Mediation – Providing a Peaceful Way to Solve Disputes" is a flier that can be put inside the student handbook. **(Template H)**
- Each student is given a "Try Peer Mediation –It Works!" poster **(Template I)**
- Posters are displayed in classrooms and around the school building. **(Template I is one example.)**
- Grade level assemblies are conducted early in the school year to discuss rules and expectations.
- Put articles about peer mediations in the school newsletter on a regular basis.
- Create a "mock mediation" video to share with the students.

Step 12. Curriculum Implementation. Provide supplemental conflict resolution education materials for teachers to use in the classrooms. (Many resources are available online for purchase.) **(Template G is an example.)**

Step 13. Facilitate Student Mediation Weekly Meetings. Weekly meetings for peer mediators are crucial in updating skills, problem solving, and team building.
- Each mediation is debriefed at the conclusion of the session. Mediators are given the opportunity to ask questions at this time.

Step 14. Keep Staff Updated. An effective program needs to be presented before the staff and student body on a regular basis.
- Provide staff members with a list of mediators.
- Provide staff members with fliers and referral forms.
- Mediation is part of the school-wide discipline plan. Information needs to be included in the staff handbook.

Step 15. Monitor and Evaluate the Program. Once the program is going, it needs supervision, support, and monitoring to keep things on track. Evaluation is a means of getting feedback for two general purposes: (1) to summarize the nature and impact of the program and (2) to change or alter the program to better serve the school.
- All mediations are processed at the end of the session.
- Peer mediators complete an evaluation form.
- Disputants complete an evaluation form.
- Regular announcements need to be given to remind the students and staff to use the mediation program.

Step 16. Celebrate. Taking time to celebrate is very important. It builds community and provides a small incentive for being a mediator.

- A celebration occurs at the end of the training.
- Certificates are presented to each student mediator. **(Template O)**
- Recognize all peer mediators at the end of the quarter and school year.
- Publish articles about the peer mediation program in the school newsletters and the area newspapers.

Step 17. Get the Parents Involved. Invite parents to participate in the mediation training, weekly meetings, or to attend the celebration ceremony.

Step 18. Review Goals and Develop Next Year's Plan. It is important to determine what works and what doesn't work, and to make adjustments, if needed.
- Program review is an ongoing process.
- It is important to publicize the peer mediation program on a regular basis.
- Continue to find ways to connect the students to their school.

Conflict Resolution Programs Reviewed

Building Your School's Conflict Management Program – Ohio Commission on Dispute Resolution & Conflict Management
Conflict Resolution/Peer Mediation (CR/PM) *Research Project* – University of Florida
The Colorado School Mediation Project. Implementing a Peer Mediation Program – Richard Cohen.
Assessing Your School's Conflict Management Program – Ohio Commission on Dispute Resolution & Conflict Management.
The Conflict Mediator's Program – Global Learning Inc. Steps in Implementing School Mediation Programs – New Mexico Center for Dispute Resolution.
Looking for Success: Evaluating Your Peer Mediation and Conflict Education Program – Tricia S. Jones. Ph.D.

Summary- Steps for Implementing a Peer Mediation Program

Initially, many conflict resolution programs were brought into schools to specifically teach students nonviolent ways to handle conflicts and reduce violence-related behaviors. Students today need to be taught that there are more effective ways of managing interpersonal conflicts than aggression or withdrawal. **Peer mediation programs are an attempt to teach students a more peaceful, problem solving approach to resolving conflicts**. Research on peer mediation programs suggests that they can have a positive impact on reducing the use of aggression in schools. Teachers are free from the time consuming task of managing conflicts between students (Fredrickson and Maruyanama). Staffs should encourage the support of the peer mediation programs, because they allow teachers to spend more time on instruction and less on classroom management; which can lead to increased academic achievement. Today, there is not "one" kind of conflict resolution program.

The research on conflict resolution and peer mediation programs indicates that:

- Conflicts among students occur frequently in schools (although the conflicts rarely result in serious injury);
- Untrained students by and large use conflict strategies that create destructive outcomes by ignoring the importance of their ongoing relationships;
- Conflict resolution and peer mediation programs seem to be effective in teaching students negotiation and mediation procedures;
- After training, students tend to use these conflict strategies, which generally lead to constructive outcomes;

- Students' success in resolving their conflicts constructively tends to result in reducing the number of student-student conflicts referred to teachers and administrators, which, in turn, tends to reduce suspensions (Johnson & Johnson).

What is a safe school?

A safe school has a positive climate where people are trusted, respected, and involved. They work together to resolve conflicts. They are not under constant stress. Students feel that adults care about them. High expectations exist so that students are successful both academically and socially. The environment of the school building determines whether or not it is a safe place.

Part 3: Ready to Use Templates A - CC

Thank you for buying this Kindle eBook, Working It Out Together!

A Step-by-Step Guide for Implementing a Peer Mediation Program

A. Staff Introduction Letter to the New Peer Mediation Program

TO: XXX STAFF
FROM: Peer Mediator Program Coordinator
DATE: XXX
RE: NEW PEER MEDIATION PROGRAM

We plan to start a Peer Mediation Program here at XX School. Peer Mediation is a program that provides a means of nonviolent conflict resolution. Students are trained as mediators who act as third party neutrals to help disputants reach agreements that are mutually satisfactory.

The selection process will begin in the next couple of weeks. All students who have at least a 2.5 G.P.A. will have the opportunity to apply to become a Peer Mediator. You will receive a list of students so you can help screen the applicants. Students can be eliminated due to poor grades, poor attendance, or the inability to stay out of conflict. Our plan is to train twenty students.

Students will conduct mediations during study hall or from classes where work can be made up. The training will consist of two half days. (Students will be expected to make up any work missed.)

Staff members may refer students to mediation by completing a referral form. (Mediation is voluntary. The student must agree to participate in mediation.) Students may refer themselves or friends to mediation. Mediations will be arranged as soon as possible.

Please let me know if you have any questions about the Peer Mediation Program. Thank you in advance for your support of this conflict resolution program.

B. Peer Mediation Flow Chart

Peer Mediation is a program designed to help students find constructive ways to resolve conflicts. With the help of trained Peer Mediators, students can learn to face problems directly, to express their feelings in a non-violent manner about another student or conflict, to resolve their conflicts in a safe and private environment, to develop skills in problem solving and to get back to learning.

The program is supported by the administration and staff at the school. To schedule a mediation, students must speak to a teacher, guidance counselor, or an administrator.

Flow Chart

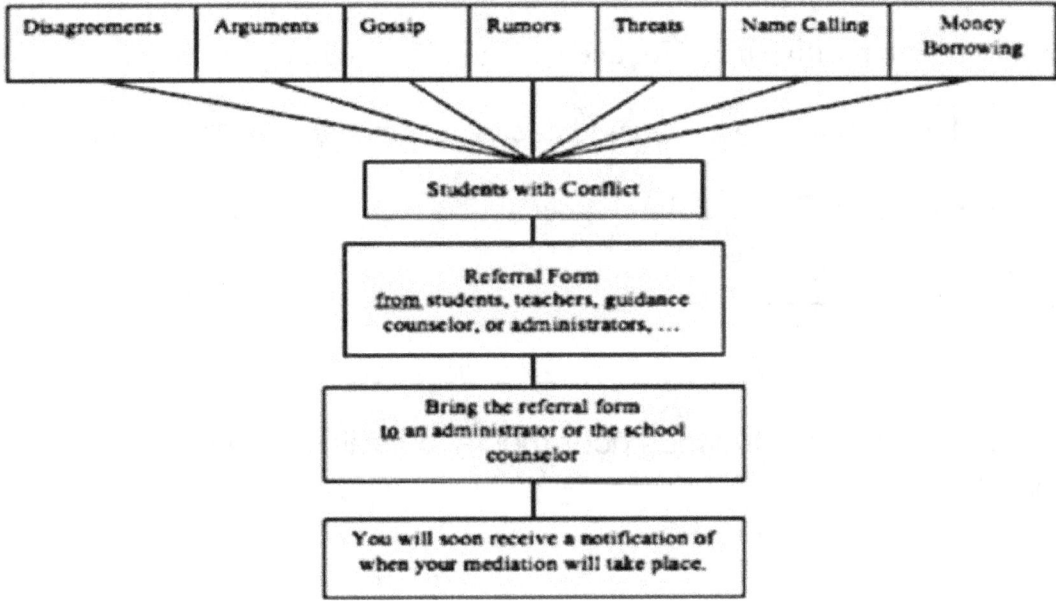

C. Peer Mediator Application

I,_____would like to become a peer mediator because
_____
_____
_____

I agree to the following:

1. Attend the peer mediation training – XX, 8:00 a.m. – 11:15 a.m., and XX , 12:00 – 3:00 p.m. (Eat 5th period both days).

2. Be willing to do mediations on a regular schedule or when I am needed for the rest of the school year.

3. Maintain positive behavior and be a good role model for others.

4. Make up any classwork missed due to peer mediator duty or training.

5. Maintain a G.P.A. of 2.5 or higher.

SIGNED: _____

DATE: _____

Have you had any previous peer mediation training? If so, what school?

D. Peer Mediator Parent Permission Letter

Dear Parents:

We are pleased to offer your son/daughter_____the opportunity to participate in the Peer Mediation Program at XX School.

The program is designed to allow specially chosen and trained students (Mediators) to help other students find positive ways to solve disagreements.

A selection process will determine which students will participate in the Peer Mediation training.

If your son/daughter has permission to participate in the Peer Mediation Program, please sign the form below and ask your child to return it to his/her homeroom teacher tomorrow.

Sincerely,

XX, Coordinator
Peer Mediation Program

PERMISSION FORM

_____has my permission to participate in the Peer Mediation Program at XX School. Training will be on XX.

_____
(Parent or Guardian's Signature)
(Date)

E. Peer Mediation Selection Process Sample Memo

TO: XX Staff
FROM: XX
DATE: XX
RE: Peer Mediator Selection Process

_____
(Staff Member's Name)

The following students have applied to become Peer Mediators. Please list your comments and/or concerns about each student you know. Please return this form to me by 3:00 on XX. **If you do not have any comments, turn in this form with your name only.** Please review "The Characteristics of a Good Mediator." Thank you for your help and support.

6th GRADE

CIERRA XX

JENNIFER XX

RICHARD XX

JULISSA XX

COURTNEY XX

Note: The names listed are not real. The first and last names of the students would be used during the actual selection process.

F. Characteristics of a Successful Mediator

CHARACTERISTICS OF A SUCCESSFUL MEDIATOR

- Successful mediator at another school
- Not shy – able to speak up
- Academically sound – will make up assignments
- Likes school
- Has good attendance
- Nurturing by nature
- Able to read, likes to read (necessary for training)
- Cooperative, reliable
- Respected by staff, students
- Will volunteer for difficult assignments
- Leadership ability
- Common sense
- Self-confident
- Respectful
- Has self-control

- Mediation is not to be used as "therapy" for the student mediator

G. Managing Conflict – Sample Support Materials

Managing Conflict: A Curriculum for Adolescents
New Mexico Center for Dispute Resolution – By Noreen Duffy Copeland

CONTENTS
Understanding Conflict
1. What is conflict?
2. What's Your Style?
3. Focus on Feelings.

Understanding Communication Skills
4. Communication Skills
5. I Have Something To Say.
6. Did You Hear What I Said?
7. Speak So Others Can Listen.
8. Listen So Others Can Speak.
9. Body Language.

Managing Anger
10. Managing Anger
11. What's Your Response?
12. Anger Activators.

Problem Solving Skills
13. Problem Solving Skills
14. Conflict in the News.
15. Actions Have Consequences.
16. Winners Fight Fair.
17. What's The Problem?

18. Putting It All Together.

H. Providing a Peaceful Way to Solve Disputes Flier

STUDENT MEDIATION
Providing a Peaceful Way to Solve Disputes

What is Mediation?
A five-phase problem solving process.
Enables students to solve their own problems.
Trained Student Mediators are present to guide the parties through the process.
Student Mediators are neutral and do not attempt to solve problems or judge.
All is confidential.

What Kinds of Conflicts are Handled Through Student Mediation?
Personal problems between people.
Probable fights.
Student related problems.

Why Try Mediation First?
Resolves problems before fighting.

Parties find their own solutions.
Resolves problems quickly.

EVERYONE WINS WHEN DISPUTES ARE SOLVED PEACEFULLY!

I. Try Peer Mediation - It Works! Poster

Having Trouble With A Classmate and Need To Talk It Out?

Request Forms are available in the main office, the counselor's office or from any teacher.

J. Congratulations Letter to Students Who Were Selected

School Name XXX
School Address

Date: XXX

Dear Student Mediator: _____

Congratulations! You have been selected to perform a very important service at your school. You will be making a big difference in the lives of many students, while gaining a valuable experience, skills, & understanding about conflict and its resolutions. This knowledge will also empower you to deal with conflicts in your own life more constructively and creatively.

Being a mediator is challenging. When individuals are involved in a conflict and can't handle it themselves, mediators act as the third person to help them talk out the problem to and come to a win/win solution. You will fight fairly. It is absolutely vital that the disputants are treated with respect and are given the opportunity to have their side of the story listened to, not only by you but by the other person involved in the conflict.

The Peer Mediation training is scheduled for:

Date: XXX   8:00 – 11:30 in the library (Eat lunch 6th period)
Date: XXX   11:00 – 3:00 in the library (Eat lunch 4th period)

Again, congratulations. We wish you success!

Name XXX, Coordinator

Peer Mediation Program

K. Rejection Letter to Students Who Were Not Selected

School Name XXX
School Address

Date: XXX

Dear:_____

We appreciate your interest in **School's Name** new Peer Mediation Program. We are pleased that you want to be a positive influence on your school.

However, due to the limited number of slots available for our training, we are unable to accept your application at this time.

Should the opportunity arise in the future, we hope that you will apply again.

Sincerely,

Name XXX, Coordinator
Peer Mediation Program

L. Peer Mediator Contract

School Name XXX
Peer Mediator Contract

As a peer mediator, I understand my role is to help students resolve conflicts peacefully. As a peer mediator, I will do my best to respect the participants of mediation, remain neutral, and keep the mediation confidential.

As a peer mediator, I agree to the following terms:
- To complete all training sessions.
- To maintain confidentiality in all mediations.
- To responsibly conduct general duties of a peer mediator, including conducting mediations, completing all necessary forms, and promoting the program.
- To maintain satisfactory school conduct (this includes requesting mediation before taking other action if I become involved in a conflict).
- To maintain satisfactory grades in all classes and make up any class work missed during training or mediation sessions.
- To serve as a peer mediator until the end of the year.

Possible actions if these responsibilities are not met are as follows:

- First Time: Warning
- Second Time: Loss of peer mediator status for one month
- Third Time: Suspension as a peer mediator

I accept these responsibilities for the school year.

Student's signature_____

Date_____

M. Peer Mediator Release Form for Student Trainers

School Name XXX

Teachers: The Peer Mediators who were trained last year have an opportunity to serve as "Trainers" when the new peer mediators are being trained. Each Peer Mediator must have permission from his/her teacher to miss class and will be responsible to make up any assignments.

The training will be:
Date: XXX   8:00 – 11:15 in the library (Eat lunch at the regular time)
Date: XXX   12:00 – 3:00 in the library (Eat lunch 5th period)

Student's Signature_____

Date_____

Period	Subject	Room #	Approval Y or N	Teacher's Signature
HR				
1st				
2nd				
3rd				
4th				
5th				
6th				
7th				
8th				
9th				

N. Peer Mediator Release Form

School Name XXX
Peer Mediator Release Form

Student_____

Grade_____ HR_____

Teachers: There are times when a peer mediator might be asked to conduct a mediation during class time. The student will be released from class **only** with your permission. Please indicate on this form if you approve an occasional release for this student.

Period	Subject	Room #	Approval Y or N	Teacher's Signature
HR				
1st				
2nd				
3rd				
4th				
5th				
6th				
7th				
8th				
9th				

O. Sample Certificate for Completing Peer Mediation Training

P. Peer Mediator Trainer Guidelines for Setting Up a Peer Mediation

PEER MEDIATOR TRAINER GUIDELINES FOR SETTING UP A PEER MEDIATION

1. When a mediation is referred to the office – an 8th grade peer mediator trainer will be selected to oversee the mediation.

2. Pick a 6th grade or 7th grade mediator to work with from the "Master Schedule" located in the Peer Mediation crate. Try to pick a mediator who hasn't had a chance to mediate (a blue folder in the front).

3. The mediator selected needs to pick another mediator to work with.

4. When the mediator has found another mediator to work with, mark off the date of the mediation by both mediators' name.

5. When you have selected your partner, look in the crate for another blue folder that says "Mediators" on the front. Then look on the purple tabs for the words that have "materials needed" on the front. Pick up one packet and take it with you.

6. The next step is to set up the room for the mediation. Mediations are to be held in the little room next to the counselor's office. Remember to put up the mediation sign on the door before the mediation begins. (Tape should be in the crate.)

7. After you have all materials, you and your partner need to decide on how you're going to divide the mediation script. Make sure both of you have a pen or a pencil to use. All of your materials should be with you when you begin the mediation.

8. Look at the referral sheet that you were given at the beginning of the mediation process; find both of the students' current location from the student locator log. The student location log will either be on the board or on the round table outside the assistant principal's office. Write each student a pass to go to the mediation. Remember to be polite and ask the teacher if the student is available. Take the students back to the mediation room. If one of the students refuses to go to mediation – remind the student that the situation can be referred to the office as a discipline issue.

9. Remember to help all 6th and 7th grade mediators fill out all the forms correctly.

10. HAVE FUN!

Q. Peer Mediations Completed Form

School Name XXX
Peer Mediations Completed
School Year 2017 - 2018

NAME	DATE 1	DATE 2	DATE 3	DATE 4
Student A				
Student B				
Student C				
Student D				
Student E				
Student F				
Student G				
Student H				
Student I				
Student J				
Student K				
Student L				
Student M				
Student N				

R. Materials Needed to Conduct a Peer Mediation

Materials Needed to Conduct a Peer Mediation

1. Request Form or Discipline Form
2. Name Badges
3. Script Packet (Includes Stop sign)
4. Mediation Observation Form
5. Peer Mediation Hall Passes (4)
6. Brainstorming List
7. Agreement Form
8. Peer Mediation Evaluation (2)
9. Disputant Evaluation (2)
10. Peer Mediation Recordkeeping Form

S. Peer Mediation Request Form

School Name XXX
Peer Mediation Request Form

Date:_____

Name of students in conflict:

1._____ **Grade**_____ **HR**_____

2._____ **Grade**_____ **HR**_____

Where conflict occurred:

_____Bus_____Classroom_____Hallway

_____Cafeteria_____Outdoors Other – Where?

Briefly describe the problem:

_____
_____
_____

Mediation requested by:

_____Student_____Teacher
_____Counselor_____Administrator

_____Other

Signature of person requesting mediation:_____

T. Peer Mediation Script - Stage I: Roles and Rules

Peer Mediation Script

Stage I: Roles and Rules

Purpose: To review roles and ground rules and get agreement to mediate.

1. Introduce yourself and tell the role of the mediator. **MY NAME IS_____, AND THIS IS_____. WE ARE YOUR MEDIATORS.**

2. Explain the mediation process. **MEDIATION IS VOLUNTARY. WE ARE NOT JUDGES. WE WILL NOT TAKE SIDES, DECIDE WHO IS RIGHT OR WRONG, OR MAKE A DECISION FOR YOU.**

   EACH OF YOU WILL HAVE A CHANCE TO TALK ABOUT THE SITUATION.

   IT IS IMPORTANT THAT YOU LISTEN CAREFULLY TO WHAT THE OTHER PERSON IS SAYING. WE WILL ASK BOTH OF YOU TO SAY/SUMMARIZE WHAT YOU HEARD THE OTHER SAY ABOUT THE SITUATION AND HOW THEY ARE FEELING ABOUT IT.

   WE WILL THEN TALK ABOUT WHAT EACH OF YOU NEEDS IN ORDER TO SOLVE THE CONFLICT AND GET A SOLUTION THAT YOU BOTH THINK IS FAIR.

AN AGREEMENT MAY BE WRITTEN AND SIGNED, IF YOU CHOOSE.

EVERYTHING THAT IS SAID HERE IS CONFIDENTIAL EXCEPT ANYTHING YOU

CHOOSE TO SHARE WITH US THAT IS ILLEGAL, OR MAY BE HARMFUL TO YOU OR SOMEONE ELSE.

3. Explain and get agreement to each of the GROUND RULES from each disputant.
   FOR MEDIATION TO WORK WE NEED YOU TO AGREE TO THESE RULES:
   * NO NAME CALLING OR PUTDOWNS
   * STAY IN YOUR CHAIRS, NO PHYSICAL FIGHTING
   * NO INTERRUPTING WHEN SOMEONE IS TALKING
   * BE AS HONEST AS YOU CAN
   * TRY TO SOLVE THE PROBLEM
   * SPEAK DIRECTLY TO THE MEDIATORS AT FIRST

   ARE THERE ANY OTHER RULES YOU NEED IN ORDER FOR MEDIATION TO WORK FOR YOU?

4. Ask if there are any questions. **DO YOU HAVE ANY QUESTIONS?**

T. Peer Mediation Script – Stage II: Hearing the Story, Gathering Information

Peer Mediation Script

Stage II: Hearing the Story, Gathering Information
Purpose: To allow each disputant to tell his/her story and express feelings

1. Ask disputants to describe how they see the situation and how they are feeling about it. **WOULD YOU TELL US WHAT HAPPENED? Or WOULD YOU DESCRIBE HOW YOU SEE THE SITUATION.**

2. Ask appropriate open-ended questions to help clarify and get more information.
   * **TELL US MORE ABOUT…**
   * And/Or **HOW LONG HAVE YOU TWO KNOWN EACH OTHER?**
   * And/Or **HOW LONG HAS THIS PROBLEM BEEN GOING ON?**

3. Restate the main points and feelings using your own words.
   * **SO YOU'RE SAYING THAT...**
   * Or **WHAT I HEAR YOU SAYING IS...**
   * Or **IT SOUNDS LIKE YOU ARE FEELING...**

Repeat Steps 1-3 with the 2nd disputant

4. Allow both disputants to respond to each other. This may happen several times in order to get all the information.
   * **WOULD YOU LIKE TO RESPOND?**
   * And/Or **WOULD YOU LIKE TO ADD ANYTHING?**

T. Peer Mediation Script - Stage III: Understanding Point of View

Peer Mediation Script

Stage III: Understanding Point of View
Purpose: To allow the disputants to understand each other's feelings and points of view.

1. Explain that you will ask both of them to say what they heard the other disputant say. Explain that understanding is different from agreeing with the other person.
   IN ORDER TO MAKE SURE THAT YOU BOTH UNDERSTAND THE OTHER'S POINT OF VIEW, WE WILL ASK YOU TO SAY OR SUMMARIZE WHAT YOU HEARD THE OTHER SAY. REMEMBER, UNDERSATNDING THE OTHER'S POINT OF VIEW DOES NOT MEAN THAT YOU AGREE.

2. Ask disputants to summarize each other's point of view and feelings about the situation.
   (1st DISPUTANT'S NAME) WOULD YOU TELL US WHAT YOU HEARD (2nd DISPUTANT'S NAME) SAY ABOUT THE SITUATION AND HOW SHE/HE IS FEELING ABOUT IT?

3. Check to make sure that what was said was heard correctly. If there was a misunderstanding, have them say again what they meant.
   (2nd DISPUTANT'S NAME) DID SHE/HE HEAR YOU CORRECTLY? IF NOT, WHAT ARE THE MOST IMPORTANT THINGS YOU WANT HIM/HER TO UNDERSTAND?

Repeat steps 2 & 3 with the other disputant

4. Summarize the main points, identifying the common issues and feelings
   * **I HEARD YOU SAY…**
   * Or **WHAT YOU ARE BOTH SAYING…**
   * Or **AS I UNDERSTAND THIS SITUATION…**

T. Peer Mediation Script - Stage IV: Finding a Solution

Peer Mediation Script

Stage IV: Finding a Solution
Purpose: To brainstorm ideas and negotiate a fair solution to the problem.

1. Explain that you will now help them to brainstorm ideas in order to find a fair solution to their situation. **WE WILL NOW BRAINSTORM IDEAS FOR A SOLUTION, ONE THAT YOU BOTH FEEL IS FAIR AND ONE THAT YOU CAN LIVE WITH. BRAINSTORMING MEANS THINKING OF AS MANY IDEAS AS YOU CAN WITHOUT JUDGING OR EVALUATING THEM. THEN WE WILL GO BACK AND SEE WHICH ONES WILL WORK FOR YOU.**

2. Ask each disputant to say what they need or what they think would be a fair solution. Encourage both disputants to give more than one idea. Playful or silly ideas are fine.
   * **WHAT IDEAS DO YOU HAVE?**
   * Or **WHAT DO YOU THINK WOULD BE A FAIR SOLUTION TO THE SITUATION?**
   * Or **WHAT DO YOU NEED IN ORDER TO SOLVE THIS SITUATION?**

3. Encourage them to come up with their own ideas. If they have difficulty thinking of something you could say:
   * **IF THIS SITUATION HAPPENED AGAIN, WHAT WOULD YOU DO DIFFERENTLY NEXT TIME TO PREVENT IT?**
   * Or **IF I WAS IN YOUR POSITION, WHAT ADVICE WOULD YOU GIVE ME?**

4. Assist disputants to negotiate a solution that is fair for both of them. **YOU HAVE SUGGESTED THE FOLLOWING IDEAS… WHICH OF THESE DO YOU THINK IS FAIR TO BOTH OF YOU?**

5. Help disputants to evaluate the solution to make sure that it is: **Realistic** – it can be done; **Specific** – it defines what, where, when, who; **Balanced** – both parties are part of the agreement. **IS THAT POSSIBLE? OR CAN YOU DO THAT?** Get specifics: **WHEN, WHERE, WHO?**

6. Summarize and restate all parts of the agreement. Check with the parties to make sure that it is accurate. **SO YOUR AGREEMENT IS THAT...**

T. Peer Mediation Script – Stage V: Writing an Agreement and Acknowledgement

Peer Mediation Script

Stage V: Writing an Agreement and Acknowledgement
Purpose: To write a fair agreement that clearly defines how terms will be carried out. To congratulate the disputants for their hard work and for reaching an agreement

1. Write the agreement in their language.

2. Read the agreement and allow for any changes, if necessary.

3. Have each party sign the agreement.
   THIS AGREEMENT IS A RECORD OF WHAT EACH OF YOU AGREES TO AND SHOWS THAT YOU ARE SERIOUS ABOUT RESOLVING THIS DISPUTE.

4. Consider and discuss the consequences of a broken agreement.

   * WHAT IF…
   * WHAT IF A MONTH FROM NOW…
   * HOW DO YOU THINK IT COULD BE HANDLED DIFFERENTLY FROM THIS TIME?

5. Remind disputants about rumors. Ask them to tell their friends that their conflict has been resolved. **TO KEEP RUMORS FROM SPREADING, WOULD YOU AGREE TO TELL YOUR FRIENDS THAT THE CONFLICT IS RESOLVED?**

6. Congratulate them on working so hard to find a fair solution to your situation/dispute.

7. The mediators may shake each disputant's hand, but should not ask the parties to shake hands. However, they may do so voluntarily.

Source: New Mexico Center for Dispute Resolution

U. STOP – Peer Mediation in Process

V. Mediation Observation Form

MEDIATION OBSERVATION FORM

GETTING READY
Learn Names of Disputants
Seating Arrangement
Review Background of Dispute
Sit Properly

STAGE 1 - OPENING
Introduction
Thank You for Choosing Mediation
Explain Mediation Roles
Explain Mediation Process
Ground Rules

STAGE 2 - DESCRIBING PROGRAM
Active Listening
Each Describes Problem and Feelings
Repeat Descriptions in Disputants Own Words

STAGE 3 - DISCUSSING PROBLEM
Disputants Talk With Each Other
Each Retells Other Side and Feelings
Consensus on Problem

STAGE 4 - FINDING A SOLUTION
Brainstorm Solutions
Evaluate Solutions
Disputants Agree on Best Solutions

STAGE 5 – CLOSING
Write the Agreement
Each Disputant Signs Agreement
Thank Disputants

W. Peer Mediation Hall Pass

Peer Mediation Hall Pass

NAME: _____

DATE: _____ TIME: _____

Peer Mediation Hall Pass

NAME: _____

DATE: _____ TIME: _____

Peer Mediation Hall Pass

NAME: _____

DATE: _____ TIME: _____

Peer Mediation Hall Pass

NAME: _____

DATE: _____ TIME: _____

Peer Mediation Hall Pass

NAME: _____

DATE: _____ TIME: _____

Peer Mediation Hall Pass

NAME: _____

DATE: _____ TIME: _____

Peer Mediation Hall Pass

NAME: _____

DATE: _____ TIME: _____

Peer Mediation Hall Pass

NAME: _____

DATE: _____ TIME: _____

X. Peer Mediation Brainstorming Worksheet

Peer Mediation Brainstorming Worksheet

List all the possible options:

- What could be done to resolve this dispute?
- What other possibilities can you think of?
- In the future, what could you do differently?

1. _____
2. _____
3. _____
4. _____
5. _____
6. _____
7. _____
8. _____
9. _____
10. _____

Y. Peer Mediation Agreement Form

Peer Mediation Agreement Form

Date _____

Briefly describe the conflict:

Mediation was: _____ successful   _____ taken seriously

_____ unsuccessful   _____ not taken seriously

Type of conflict: _____ Rumor _____ Threat _____ Name-calling

_____ Fighting _____ Loss of property _____ Other_____

The students whose signatures appear below met with a peer mediator and with the assistance of the mediator reached the following agreement.

Disputant_____

Agrees to_____

Disputant _____

Agrees to_____

We have made and signed this agreement because we believe it resolves the issue(s) between us.

_____   _____
Disputant's Signature   Disputant's Signature

_____   _____
Peer Mediator's Signature   Peer Mediator's Signature

Length of mediation (minutes)_____

Z. Peer Mediator Evaluation Form

Peer Mediator Evaluation Form

Name:_____

Date:_____

Description of Conflict:_____

1. This was a successful mediation.   YES   NO

2. I felt comfortable mediating.   YES   NO

3. The disputants understood the process.   YES   NO

4. The disputants will use this process again.   YES   NO

5. I did a good job mediating because_____
_____

6. I could do a better job next time by _____
_____

7. I remained impartial.   YES   NO

AA. Disputant Immediate Follow-Up Form

Disputant Immediate Follow-Up Form
Please answer the following questions now by circling your answer.

Student Name: _____ HR _____

1. Was a written agreement reached in mediation?
   YES   NO

2. Was the mediation conducted fairly?
   YES   NO   SOMEWHAT

3. Do you feel that the original problem that brought you to mediation has been settled?
   YES   NO   PARTIALLY

4. Do you feel the mediator took sides?
   YES   NO

5. Would you use mediation again to try to resolve a dispute?
   YES   NO   MAYBE

6. Were you satisfied with the outcome of your mediation?
   YES   NO

7. Do you think this mediation will make a difference in the way you and the other person(s) get along?
   YES   NO   MAYBE

8. Do you feel the mediator took your concerns seriously.
   YES   NO

9. Overall, how successful would you say your mediation was?
   Successful   Partially Successful   Not Successful

BB. Peer Mediation Record Keeping Form

Month_____   Page _____ Of _____

#	Grade	Sex	Race	Loc.	Req. By	Type	Time	Signed (Y/N)
1.								
2.								
3.								
4.								
5.								
6.								
7.								
8.								
9.								
10.								

KEY

Location
B = Bus
R = Classroom
H = Hallway
C = Cafeteria
D = Outdoors
O = Other

Requested By
S = Student
T = Teacher
C = Counselor
A = Administrator
O = Other

Type
R = Rumor
T = Threat
N = Name Calling
F = Fighting/Hitting
P = Property Loss/Damage
O = Other

Race
1 - Caucasian
2 – African American
3 - Other

Time (to the nearest 5 minutes)

Signed (Was an agreement signed?)

CC. Peer Mediator Business Cards

Got Conflict?
Peer Mediation can help you solve your conflict!

Work It Out Together!

Got Conflict?
Peer Mediation can help you solve your conflict!

Work It Out Together!

Got Conflict?
Peer Mediation can help you solve your conflict!

Work It Out Together!

Got Conflict?
Peer Mediation can help you solve your conflict!

Work It Out Together!

Got Conflict?
Peer Mediation can help you solve your conflict!

Work It Out Together!

Got Conflict?
Peer Mediation can help you solve your conflict!

Work It Out Together!

Got Conflict?
Peer Mediation can help you solve your conflict!

Work It Out Together!

Got Conflict?
Peer Mediation can help you solve your conflict!

Work It Out Together!

www.ingramcontent.com/pod-product-compliance
Lightning Source LLC
Chambersburg PA
CBHW080940220526
45465CB00008BA/3101